QUEER CHRISTMAS IN COWTOWN

YYC QUEER WRITERS
CURATED BY M. JANE COLETTE

QUEER CHRISTMAS IN COWTOWN
13 queer shorts for the 12 days of Christmas
by YYC Queer Writers
curated by M. Jane Colette
photography by Tet Millare

These stories may or may not be true. Let's all agree, though, for the sake of legalities, that they are all works of imagination and fiction. The names, characters, and incidents portrayed in them are the work of the authors' imagination. Any resemblance to actual persons, living or dead, events or localities is entirely coincidental. Completely. Especially any references to you. We're not not talking about you. Well, maybe we are. No, we're not! We're not!

*Published in collaboration with M. Jane Colette
& YYC Queer Writers by
GENRES were made to be BROKEN
121, 104-1240 Kensington Rd NW
Calgary, Alberta T2N3P7 Canada*

For all the queer, unique snowflakes in our lives

CONTENTS

INSTRUCTIONS, FOR THE WRITERS

FROM M. JANE COLETTE

*H*ello, Bold Queer Writer!
You are hereby cordially invited to queer up *YYC* this Christmas. Ready?

Statement: TLDR. Short version?

Retort: Write something queer. Christmas or winter themed. Loosely associated with Calgary. Memoir/non-fiction style preferred, but you can lie—er, fictionalize —if it *sounds* true.

The Project: *Queer Christmas In Cowtown*, an anthology of Christmas-themed stories by YYC Queer Writers, curated by M. Jane Colette, and published by GENRES were made to be BROKEN

Question: Only Christmas?

Answer: Other December-occurring holidays welcome, if you wanna play with Hanukkah, Winter Solstice, Kwanzaa, or, heck, New Year's for that matter. No Valentine's Day, Easter or Halloween, though, ok? If you have a Ramadan story that takes place in December, bring it on.

Question: It's a December story, but not really a Christmas story. Is that ok?

Answer: Read on...

Your task: To write a non-fictional, memoir-or-some-thing-like-it style piece that somehow or other touches on Christmas / December / holidays. And queerness. Pretty broad umbrella, right? Let's narrow it a little. Must be PROSE. NO POETRY in this one. (Sorry, poets. But poems are welcome in our second annual *Screw Chocolate* project.)

Question: How long?

Answer: As short as you like if it's brilliant. No longer than 1500 words.

Exclamation: What?

Answer: 1500 words. You audience (and your editor) has a short-attention span. Write tight. Write short. Write snappy.

Question: How queer does it have to be?

Answer: Duh. As queer as you. No more, no less.

Question: How Calgary does it have to be?

Answer: Meh. So long as the writer's from Calgary, you can set your story in Paris if you really want to. Although... top billing will go to the story that incorporates cowboy boots and a branding iron into a narrative that situates the story firmly in Cowtown. Maybe. Unless the Paris-set story is really good.

Question: Who chooses and edits the stories?

Answer: Me.

Question: Why the fuck you?

Answer: I get shit done. It's, like, my motto.

Question: Who gets the money?

Answer: Ha ha ha ha ha ha ha, darling, you know nothing about publishing. You're doing it or love and glory, baby, as am I. All and any royalties/profits from the project will be donated to Camp fYrefly.

WANT TO BE part of this project next year? Check *mjanecolette.com/QueerChristmas* for details.

mjanecolette

INSTRUCTIONS, FOR THE READERS

FROM M. JANE COLETTE

*R*ead.
      Enjoy.

Um... I have a feeling you expect more. Yes? An overview of what's inside?

A baker's dozen of queer Christmas stories for the twelve days of Christmas. An exercise in writing—storytelling—story *finishing*—and story sharing.

The writers were asked to write "true" and "queer." (Also, short. Because, shiny things!) Their interpretations of these instructions are as marvellously unique—and queer—and true—as they are.

So... Read. Enjoy.

And... join us? Tell your own truth, your own story.

And share it.

Stories—queer, true, *shared*—are how we're going to change the world.

Truth.

QUEER AS FUCK ANGLICAN VIRGINAL, IN TWO DRAFTS

BY DALLAS BARNES

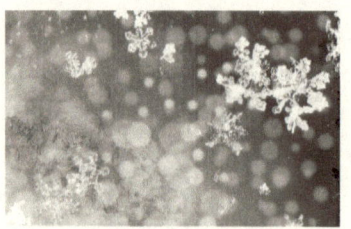

*C*hristmas. Everything about it is queer. Isn't it?

I. CLEAN DRAFT

When I was born, my mom declared that I would be Anglican. Was it because she had a deep desire for me to be closer to God? Did she wish for some divine guidance in my life from the Lord and Saviour?

My guess is, no.

As I understand it, being Anglican was just the way her family... was. We were all descendants of a British middle-class dynasty of servants, fishermen, and house-wives. Being Anglican was the way of the Brits, and as my mom always said, "We are just like Catholics, but we can get divorced."

Divine tenets for sure!

Christmas as a questioning queer kid in the 80s was brilliant. Presents were aplenty, gossip was abundant, and the food was ample. I had no understanding of what Christmas was—for all I knew, it was the celebration of Santa's birth.

I think I had been to church and Sunday School a handful of times as a result of my mom's intermittent attempts to enlighten me in the ways of the Anglican faith. All I got out of it was an understanding that Jesus made squirrels out of pinecones.

Odd, I know, and completely untrue, but the pinecones, squirrels, and Jesus imprinted on my tiny and obviously misguided brain.

As I drifted into my twenties, the pinecone-squirrel-Jesus associations got more complicated, as I struggled to understand why and how we do things as a society:

- Why was I expected to marry a man?
- Why did my dad say that secretarial school was the best alternative for me?
- Why was I always ashamed of my body?
- Why in God's name did I celebrate Christmas when I had no love for organized religion?
- And why did I still want to celebrate it?

Fast-forward to the year 2007. I was 34 years old. I declared my queerness publicly, and I had U-hauled everything I owned (two angry cats included) from Vancouver to Calgary to start a new life of queer utopia.

The consequences of this new start included complete and utter poverty, and my first Christmas away from my dysfunctional and constant family unit.

It should have been thrilling. Not the poverty—the Christmas away from family. By 2007, my parents had divorced after more than 30 years of marriage. There'd be no dreamy childhood Christmas for me even if I stayed in Vancouver. But as Christmas approached, the brand new prairie girl that I was would have taken anything familiar, no matter how dysfunctional.

Everything around me was different... and I was scared.

I made some fantastic friends in Calgary. I finally felt like I belonged to something I had never experienced in Vancouver. I was surrounded with queerness, and up to my ears in beautiful dykedom. I had hooked up with some amazing hotties, cried over lost loves and friends with like-minded chicks, and line-danced with the queerest of cowfolk.

Life was amazing.

I was the happiest I had ever been—ever.

Yet—that Christmas, I was alone. I was still that questioning homo with a penchant for understanding things unexplained. I still didn't get why Christmas meant so much to me. I had a hard time spending more than a minute or two with each family member, let alone all of them at once. I was stuck between my queer Garden of Eden, and the longing for a place in rainy Vancouver with a family only a psychopath could love.

When I was that queer, questioning, kid, I counted

down the days until Santa made his arrival. I figured out the actual Santa myth by the time I was five (the curse of having teenage friends on the same block as me), but I didn't want to tell my mom for two reasons: I did not want to hurt her feelings; and, the presents I got from Santa were by far superior to anything else I received. The wrapping paper was always shiny and foily—and I wasn't about to pass that up.

The anticipation of the day of ultimate consumerist consumption was highlighted in red pen, glitter, and highlighter on my calendar. I started crossing off the days as early as July. I had a long sheet of foolscap thumbtacked to my wall with each date from July to December 25 listed, a day per line. Beginning July 1, I crossed off each of those dates, every damn day.

As I got older, the foolscap disappeared. But the excitement didn't. Even when I moved out on my own, my dad would pick me up at the crack of dawn so that I would be home for Christmas breakfast. When my parents separated, I made it work by hanging with my dad during the day, and then having vegetarian lasagna in the evening with my mom and her friend at her tiny little apartment.

As time passed—as my grandparents passed away, as my parents' divorce became the new normal—the situation slowly changed.

The present tally declined.

Yet... the excitement remained.

And then, I moved to Calgary.

The comforts of dysfunctional Anglican holidays provided some sort of stability to this non-religious girl. The freedom of being all sorts of queer without any reminders of a life where I felt I did not belong offered a different kind of normal. Not to be deemed a quitter, I was determined to make a go of what Calgary had to offer that Christmas.

I let everyone I knew know that I would be home, alone, that December 25th.

I waited for the onslaught of invites.

Most of my friends were going home for Christmas.

I waited some more.

Still nothing.

And then, like an affirmation from God herself, I was invited to a queer, orphan Christmas.

The day was full. The atmosphere drunk, queer, and warm. There was ham, turkey, chips, cheese, beer, sporadic make-outs, and wicked come-ons. It was a winter wonderland of women. Woot! There was no mom, no dad, very little dysfunction, and lots of queer. It wasn't the Christmas I knew, but it was the Christmas I didn't know I needed.

As more Christmases without the Vancouver crowd came and went, the level of excitement, longing, and unreal expectations slowly faded. I can't say it is just like any other day because it isn't. It ranks slightly above that.

But there is no shiny and foily wrapping paper magic.

What my first Christmas away from home taught me was that sometimes, memories are just that—memories. The days of gifts abound, and magical turkeys are no more. I can attempt to recapture these memories with the tools that I have today, or just resign to the fact that this Anglican (I guess Catholic? Catholics probably have dibs on Christmas, right?) creation is not mine anymore. Is this a part of growing up? Possibly, or maybe it is just an acceptance that what's done is done.

So thank you, Anglicanism, for providing me with memories of magic.

What does that mean?

My queer Christmas means no Christmas at all.

No, scratch that. My queerness means that Christmas, still, always, maybe forever, is being redefined.

2. ROUGH DRAFT

It's funny that the terms "queer" and "Christmas" are a subject, let alone an experience for some.

I had a queer Christmas once. It was 2007, and I had just moved to Calgary from my 34 year existence in Vancouver. In actuality it was my first Christmas away from home – ever.

Rosalyn/Dustin

Lyn

Ham with the pineapple and cherries

Lots of alcohol

Tshirt from las vegas

Expensive perfume

Smurfs

Taxi super early

Called parents

Drinks

Weird dyke flirting

A first of its kind for me

Dallas Barnes is a queer, cisgender, feminist, activist, and writer. She writes about life—its downfalls, turmoils, hilarities, and elations. Her experience with mental illness and all things queer makes her writing real, raw, and in your face. Dallas lives in Calgary, Alberta with her cat Grizzly and tweets as @salladsenrab.

EDITOR'S NOTE: I asked Dallas to let us publish her rough draft alongside her clean draft, because I felt it offered such great insight—and I hope inspiration and instruction—on how a story comes to be. Along the way you lose the Smurfs, say, and the super early taxi—but you remember your first Christmas and Jesus making squirrels out of pinecones, and your parents' divorce, and grandma dying, and bang. There's your narrative.

THE NAME

BY NOLA SARINA

I tuck the last candy cane inside the stocking and hang it up on the mantle. I stare at the colours, and the names embroidered on the fabric. I wish I'd known I had it all wrong last year.

Oops, forgot one chocolate kiss. I slip it down into the stocking and tug the edges to make sure all the treasures inside are concealed. My son needs this stocking to be just right this year. As desperately as he needs my love, my support, my structure, my validation. This isn't just some decoration, nor some aesthetic preference. This blue stocking is twelve dollars and ninety-seven cents, plus six dollars worth of embroidery that will, in his eyes, equal a million. The best Christmas ever. His *first* Christmas, in a way.

The backing peels effortlessly from the snowflake-patterned bow, and I stick it down, right on top of the teddy bear's head, its arms dangling over the furry edge of the stocking. Two blue, overstuffed, giant socks. One pink. I stare at the packages beneath the tree. I love it all: their garish colours, the snowmen and reindeer, the ribbons, and the glitter that's covering them as it falls from a decoration above.

A smile forms on my lips.

I know it's only a stocking.

But tomorrow, when my son wakes up and rushes out of his room to see what Santa brought, he will feel like every other boy who celebrates Christmas. He won't find pink ribbons and matching sister necklaces adorning his stocking and have to fake a smile, while watching his brother tear into gifts he hasn't dared to ask for yet. He won't see a name that doesn't match his soul embroidered on the fur. No one will expect things from him that make him feel like he's wrong, inside.

He's not wrong. He was never wrong. Only *we* were wrong, when we assumed he was a girl and never bothered to look close enough to see that with every dress we hoped he'd want to wear, every use of his birth name, every time we said *she*, he was screaming inside with a pain he didn't have words to name. The pain of not being able to be what everyone told him he should be. The pain of feeling broken, backwards, unlovable.

That's the only part he was wrong about. He's not broken, backwards, or unlovable. He's just... a boy.

I lean forward, uncap the marker with my teeth, and

scrawl his name in big, bold letters right across the smiling Santa on the paper of one of his gifts. Not the name I gave him before he was born, that he carried like a burden for eight years. A name that fits him, that we chose together as I learned how to call him my son. I write it again and again, on every gift that belongs to him, bigger, bolder, with hearts and smiley faces beside each one, the ink shouting his name with gratitude and pride.

Tomorrow morning, he will see the stocking with that name and know that I understand, now. I finally know who he is. He will see that I believe him, that I trust him, that I love him. He's my son, and he always has been, even when I didn't understand who he was.

My hands close around the hot ceramic of a mug of hot cider, spiced heartily from hours of simmering on the stove with a cinnamon stick. The twinkling from the bulbs on the tree casts starlight across the floor of my midnight-silent house. Not a single present under the tree bears my name.

But I don't need any presents. I've got the best gift of all, this year. My child—my beautiful child—somehow found the strength to tell me he knew himself better than we did. And in that moment, my heart bloomed with a cacophonic blur of joy and sorrow. Joy, that my child trusted me enough to tell me I hadn't really been listening to him. Sorrow, that I'd not seen it sooner, not known there was a way I could help him feel okay. Validated. Heard. Accepted. Celebrated for everything that he is and always has been, even when we didn't know we had to look deeper than his skin.

My only gift, this year, is knowing with every ray of my soul that my children trust that they are loved.

Steam from the cider touches my lips, and I breathe the scent deeply, imagining the excitement that will wake me in just a few short hours of snowfall.

I can't wait for Christmas morning.

Nola Sarina is a paranormal romance, dark fantasy, and erotica author from Alberta, Canada. She loves weaving romances that leave you breathless and challenge typical relationships with the most mind-blowing twists.

Represented by Michelle Johnson of Inklings Literary Agency, Nola is the author of the spicy hot dark fantasy Vesper series. She is also the co-author of Wild Hyacinthe and THE CORE with friend Emily Faith. THE CORE invites every reader to throw stereotypes out the window, strip down, and get dirty.

Follow Nola on Twitter @nolasarina.

DOUBLE TRANSITION

BY BEATRICE AUCOIN

"I want to keep my breasts," I blurted out to my spouse, Brett, as we crossed the street from the doctor's office with our five-year-old son, Sam, in tow in a bright red wagon. The English major part of me was angry at the blue sunny sky and warm autumnal temperature of this December day: I just learned I had breast cancer and didn't have any hint of a pathetic fallacy in my Calgary foothills surroundings to help me feel the slightest bit better.

It was easier to be angry at that than to feel the numbness radiating into my core from the grape-sized lump sitting at the top of my left breast. I had brushed across it a few weeks before as I was nestling into bed with a favourite book. What was that? It couldn't be cancer: I'm a thirty-something active vegetarian who doesn't smoke or drink.

But the biopsy results came back with cancer.

Cancer. Cancer. Cancer.

My spouse was reassuring and practical: "Let's talk to the breast surgeon first."

Our home was festooned with Sam's crayon drawings of railroad crossings, which he drew by the dozen, as they were among his favourite things. I was always drawn to a red group of three railroad crossings, in different sizes and with unique features, in one picture in particular. Sam had labelled it "three" in his kindergarten scrawl. It made me think of our little family. We were ourselves and all belonged together.

But who was I without my breasts? I had always been the smart, quiet woman with big breasts who liked to read. These pieces of my body, protruding from my chest since I was nine, had defined so much of who I was for most of my life: everything from being catcalled as a little girl to feeding my child.

I knew better, of course, than to define womanhood by body parts. I had friends and family of a variety of genders; body parts or their absence does not define a gender. My breasts, however, had defined much of my feminine gender for so long that I didn't know what I would do once they weren't part of me.

A few weeks later, Brett and I met with my Foothills Hospital breast surgeon, who presented my breast cancer treatment choices to me based on his diagnosis of stage 0 ductal carcinoma *in situ*. My best medical choice for preventing reoccurrence, for survival, and to stay here with my family was to have a double mastectomy. And that's what I told Brett as we had pizza together afterward: "I'm going to have my breasts removed and have reconstruction."

My spouse squeezed my hand and said, "I support your choice."

"I'm transgender," Brett told me that evening.

We were still upbeat from our meeting with the breast surgeon. I was even thinking about doing some Christmas baking of melted chocolate and pomegranate seeds, which had been a yummy hit last year in our house. My prognosis wasn't looking quite so scary because I believed it'd be one surgery in the new year to get rid of this cancer and I'd be done. (As it turned out, the diagnosis was incorrect; I actually had stage 3a invasive ductal carcinoma, but that's a story for another day.)

Now all thoughts of baking fled from my mind as I looked at my spouse telling me her truth.

Brett's complete candour is one of the qualities I've always admired about her. She was open about being bi to me during the entire course of our relationship and initially thought certain feminine traits she possessed were the result of her being bi. And then some speculation about gender identity led to Brett coming out as genderqueer two years before my cancer was diagnosed. My reaction to Brett's journey was always, "That's awesome!" I loved that Brett was completely comfortable exploring questions of sexuality and gender identity. I loved seeing her adopt a more feminine appearance.

I have always known that despite appearing hetero to the world, this label didn't apply to me. I was into certain types of women and men and in my 30s felt most comfortable with describing myself as queer. Going along with my husband, now wife, to wherever life took us has been part of what we have done for over a decade.

However, a small part of me was nervous. I knew I wanted to stay with her. The things I loved most about her were the same and would always be the same no matter what: she was intelligent, a great parent to our son, an avid cyclist, a follower of Canadian politics, passionate about post-secondary education, and both a fun and excellent companion to go with hand-in-hand through life. But would Brett undergoing this transition affect our love and attraction for each other?

Brett's input into my decision about my body and health earlier that day had been nothing but unqualified support.

I support your choice.

And I knew then, whatever happened with how Brett presented her gender identity, I would love and find her as attractive as ever. There was no doubt in her heart that

I would be just as beautiful to her without my breasts. There was no doubt in my heart that she would be just as beautiful to me appearing as the woman she has always been.

So I told her that I love her and I would support her; our son and I would be with her on this journey. Just as I had to do what was best for my well-being in dealing with my cancer, Brett needed to do what was best to express her gender identity.

Brett and I held each other and cried. We cried for the harshness of me having to deal with breast cancer at a young age. We cried for Brett putting words to a beautiful truth she had come to after a long period of introspection. We knew, whatever challenges the future might hold for one of us going through breast cancer and the other a gender transition at the same time, we would be together going along to wherever life would take us.

Beatrice Aucoin is a breast cancer survivor and queer writer originally from Cape Breton. She makes her home in downtown Calgary with her wife, Brett Bergie, and their son, Sam.

EDITOR'S COMMENT: Holy fuck. That's all I've got to say. You don't believe in miracles and true love? Read this story again.

A BED FOR ANDI

BY L. SARA BYSTERVELD

*O*n Andi's first visit to my parents' house, for my birthday in September 2013, my husband and I presented her as a friend to whom I wanted to show my parents' ranch (not in Cowtown, but proximal to an *actual* cow town). We left it at that, but found ourselves put on the spot when, around 9 pm, the conversation turned to bedtime. It was already late enough that we had grown hopeful that my parents wouldn't ask where Andi would be sleeping and we could just slip her into our room without question. But, it was time for our daughter to go to bed, and this brought up questions.

Mom: So if Neko is going to bed, should we set up a bed for her on the floor in your room so that Andi can sleep in the spare room?

The three of us: <deer in headlights eyes>

Me: Um no, that's okay, we're going to bed late, so we'd wake Neko up. Andi can sleep on the floor in our room.

Dad: Are you sure?

Andi: Yeah, that'll be fine.

She slept in the full-sized bed with us and in the morning we messed up the floor bed to give it the appearance of having been used in case they came into the bedroom at any point.

Three months later, when Andi arrived at my parents' place for Christmas, it had been:

- eight months since Andi and I started dating;
- six months since we fell in love;
- four months since we began shakily forming a triad with our male partner, my husband who was now also Andi's boyfriend, Justan;
- three months since that first visit.

It would be another nine months before I would write

my parents an email explaining to them that I am, in fact, bisexual and that Andi is, in fact my... actually, *our* girlfriend. That we are in this for the long haul, that we're committed, and that even if we broke up, *I* would still be bisexual.

When Andi drove up the snowy driveway to their house on December 27, there was a fire in the wood stove, coffee in the pot, and gifts under the tree, though none for Andi. Justan and I had a stack of gifts for her, but how could we have explained that? They were hidden in the car, to be opened later in our room, where the decoy bed was already made on the floor.

Family dinner that night was the traditional lasagna and salads my mom's side adopted years ago as a break from turkey. Not that I needed the break any longer, since we had been estranged from my dad's side of the family for a few years so that was one less Christmas dinner for us. Justan's mom made ham. I don't eat ham. I do love lasagna.

Aunts, uncles, and cousins filed in carrying layered salads, and we introduced Andi to each group as they arrived: "This is our friend. Andi." We already knew that if we stayed together much longer, a better explanation would be needed. Although my parents were happy enough to beat around the bush, most of my mom's side of the family was straightforward, even blunt. If we didn't tell them, they would ask.

People see what they want to see. Because of this truth, some members of my family (a conservative farming family from rural Alberta) saw my relationship with Andi for what it was—romantic love—and others saw what we let them believe—friendship.

I'm not sure what my parents saw. Likely, they could have easily guessed what was up. Just as likely, they had no desire to know nor to admit to themselves what was happening. I love my parents very much, and would even say we're close, but we're close in a certain way. We speak on the phone often, enjoy one another's company, are kind to one another and make each other laugh, but I don't share intimate details or struggles with them.

Our relationship seems to function well that way, and that's why I later chose to come out to them in an email rather than face-to-face or even on the phone. Speaking frankly about our personal lives was not the norm for us, and it would have felt terribly awkward, if not impossible, for me to get the words out.

I also wanted to give them time and space to process, and then approach me with any questions they might have, if they chose to.

I've often wondered whether bi-invisibility—the ability of a bisexual person to blend in with either gay or straight communities depending on the gender of their partner—is a blessing or a curse. I've spent years feeling guilty about "passing" as straight. I've been with Justan since I was 18. I've had girlfriends and friends with benefits since then, but to most people I have always appeared pretty straight. Only within the past few years have fellow bisexual friends helped me recognize that I don't need to feel guilty, and that passing isn't a privilege—it's something that causes suffering and that I have suffered because of passing. I haven't been acknowledged for who

I am, I have had to live under people's assumptions, and I haven't felt truly a part of the queer community even though I am.

Looking back, it does seem strange for someone who is bisexual to identify as only an ally when their letter is right there in the acronym.

Although I couldn't yet tell my parents about the relationship that was forming between the three of us, it meant so much for me to have Andi there at my parents' place for Christmas. I couldn't wait for her to bond with my parents, for the three of them to get to know each other. I hoped that if they knew her, liked her, it would be an easier adjustment for them once I finally had to come out.

After we had eaten dinner that first Christmas, and everyone had opened their gifts (everyone but Andi), the three of us sat on the loveseat together near the front door as my aunts, uncles, and cousins said their good-byes. We sat close. We smiled at each other. One of my aunts watched us, lingering a bit too long, and smiled knowingly. Whatever the story she was forming in her head, she was pleased with it.

The next Christmas, she would draw Justan in the Christmas draw and have a special Christmas ornament made for us, featuring three snowmen labelled "Lindsay," "Justan," and "Andi." Sometimes gleeful support means a lot, compared to quiet acceptance or tolerance.

L. Sara Bysterveld answers to Lindsay (her very good reason for the pretentious pen name can be found on her author site, LSaraBysterveld.com), aside from when she doesn't answer at all because she is hiding from her five kids/step-kids, two partners, and two cats. She was voted 'Most Likely to Publish a Book' and 'Most Likely to Be a Syndicated Columnist' by her peers at her college journalism graduation party, immediately before jumping into the pool fully clothed. She's currently working on the former with her non-fiction book, Triads: How It Works When Love Includes Three. *Find out more about triads and the book on Instagram (@thetriadbook) or the website TheTriadBook.com.*

EXCEPT FOR YOU

BY LOTIS CERVANTES

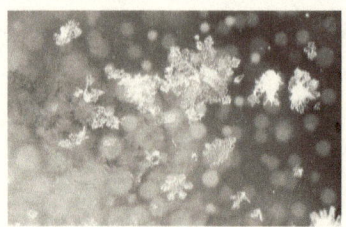

*E*verything is ready.

The huge tree, decorated and alight, stands in the corner of the living room, boxes of gifts stacked underneath, waiting to be opened.

The house, with nary a shadow of dirt or dust, is open and bright, waiting for the arrival of old and new friends alike.

Christmas music plays in the background, stirring memories of holidays spent with families on another side of the world.

My roommates and I are getting ready for the party, pushing thoughts of melancholy away from our minds.

Everything is ready.

There is only one thing missing.

My would-be-wife is not here.

She is in California, spending the holidays with her family.

For the most part, this is how we are going to spend Christmas or any important event for that matter—on Skype, wishing we could be together.

Dreaming.

We talk for hours while she watches me get ready.

She's in her living room, the cat sitting on her lap.

Our conversations are punctuated with *I miss you... I wish I was there... I love you...*

I touch the computer screen, hoping my warmth will somehow be transmitted. But it's just wishful thinking.

The laptop has fingerprints all over it, evidence of the longing that has to wait till our next meeting.

Hold on.

Stay strong.

We'll be together soon.

"Soon" is days, weeks, months, and if we're unlucky, years away.

The unavoidable challenges of being in a long distance relationship are aggravated by the uncertainty of immigration and a temporary status in a new country.

I can't go anywhere.

My not-yet-wife is the only one who can visit.

I lose count of the tears I shed.

But I am hopeful, and so is she.

"We'll be together soon," she repeats.

I nod, smile, agree.

"I should go. Talk to you tomorrow?" I say to her while I check my reflection in the camera.

"Don't leave me yet," she pleads.

I stay till one of my roommates calls from upstairs.

We have never-ending goodbyes till one gives the signal that they really must go. This time, it's me.

I blow her a kiss and end the conversation, my heart heavy.

When I leave my room, I put on a smile.

My roommates cheer when they see me coming up the stairs.

I look at their faces.

We all share the same predicament. The people we most love... aren't physically here.

And so, every joy of Christmas comes tinged with pain.

But, despite the sadness Christmas brings, we know how to celebrate.

Everything is ready. The tree sparkles. The house is waiting for the arrival of our friends.

You are not here. But you will be.

Soon.

Lotis Clemente Cervantes dreamed of a white Christmas but never thought it would come true till she moved to Calgary from the Philippines. She loves her new home except when she's ankle deep in the snow. You can check out her works at lcervantes@wattpad.com. She sometimes tweets as @quinncelement37.

CRUSHING

BY T

 y skis are scraping powder off grey boulders as I slide hip-heavy down the rock face. He waits at the bottom, supervising with a grin. Teasing me as I bend in all the wrong ways. When I finally maneuver the neon green beans attached to my feet over the ledge, I plop off a rock wall and into the soft runoff of a high mountain crevasse.

"Crushin' it!" Old Friend fist bumps me.

He is standing over me, bright sunshine against overcast skies and the flat blue glow of distant mountain tops in the afternoon. I wouldn't be here in this moment without his sense of adventure; I wouldn't be in this untouched country trusting that I am strong enough to get there without his unapologetic enthusiasm. We are, briefly, alone, silence in between marbled walls settling onto us and the cold goose down I'm lying against. The crisp air thickens and slows and he is looking at me and he is so rugged and so strong and so different and I just want him to kiss me.

Then the next head pops over the ledge. He yells instructions and I scoot out of the way and the moment is gone. When I explode in the powder a minute later, losing skis and sinking to my waist, all I can think about is him and how cute it is that he keeps checking on me and how I love that he smiles whenever he looks back.

Damn, T is crushin' hard.

Dear Santa, T's still crushing hard. Could you, would you? Thanks. See who else is on her wish list at boysboysboysandt.wordpress.com.

EDITOR'S CONFESSION: T is one of my favourite writerly discoveries this year, and I really hope to shake her out of her too-secretive pseudonym... or at least into some longer pieces... soon. Stay tuned.

RIBBONS

BY ALYSSA LINN PALMER

The closest I ever got to a truly queer Christmas gift was when a friend of mine suggested I should be trussed up naked in ribbons and left for his girlfriend to find.

It didn't happen, obviously. Lack of will, lack of... *cajones*? Truly, a lack of a real interest on my part in his girlfriend, knowing it was just *his* interest in seeing something that could have been porn in "real life." Not really a good motivator, at least not for me.

Back to seeming straight, to bi-erasure, to passing. Easier, yes, but frustrating.

It was almost Christmas when I finally told my

parents that if I got married, it might as likely be to a woman as to a man, depending on who I fell in love with.

Did they know before? I have no idea. Maybe, maybe not. I didn't pass then.

I'm closer now to getting married than I ever have been in my life (except maybe once, but I was barely eighteen... I'll get to that shortly), and I know that if I do, I'll continue to pass. As Anna Paquin once told Larry King, bisexuality doesn't disappear if you're married to someone of the opposite sex.

(The first brush with possible marriage, I was barely eighteen, and it was New Year's Eve. Almost Christmas. Absolutely freezing cold when he asked me on the steps of the pub just before midnight. Strong feelings, but too young to take that step.)

Love is a person, not a gender. It took me a long while to figure that out. This Christmas, it'll be love. Love is love is love is love is love is love is love is love. Ribbons optional, but what a tempting gift.

Alyssa Linn Palmer *writes mostly dark romantic fiction, but when she isn't, her work is happy and bright. Find her at @alyslinn on Twitter & Instagram, and find links to her books at AlyssaLinnPalmer.com.*

THERAPY

BY M. JANE COLETTE

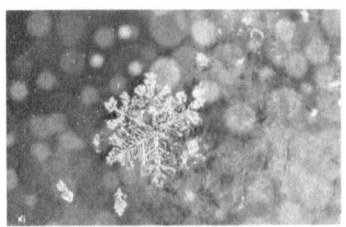

herapist: So. Do you want to talk about your Christmas issues?

Jane: I don't have Christmas issues.

Therapist: You do.

Jane: I don't.

Therapist: Jane, I've read your books. The first one actually has a chapter called "Worst Christmas Ever." In the second one, the cataclysmic climax occurs at Christmas Dinner...

Jane: Actually, they make it through dinner fine. The explosion comes after...

Therapist: Splitting hairs. Christmas issues. You. Severe. Shall we talk about them?

Jane: No.

Therapist: Is this going to be another one of those sessions where you stare at me belligerently and, at the end, say, "I don't know why I pay for this shit?"

Jane: Yes.

Therapist: Have you considered that this relationship isn't working and that you should get another therapist?

Jane: No. I like you. And I'm just starting to get used to you.

Therapist: So, perhaps by next Christmas, we will delve into your Christmas issues?

Jane: Don't hold your breath.

We fall silent, and I stare at the space just to the left of her ear. Not belligerently. But then I frown. Why did she say that? Bitch. I am not belligerent. I just have a very heightened sense of privacy. And she—who is she? A total stranger. However many degrees in listening to people bitch and whine about their shit she has hanging on her walls, she has not earned the right to hear my neuroses. No matter how much I'm paying her.

I shift my gaze from the space beside her left ear to her actual ear. Then to her eyes.

Belligerently.

Therapist: Belligerently.

Jane: Have you considered that maybe you're just not that good at your job?

Therapist: Oh, Jane.

When she says my name, she sounds like my grade seven teacher, Mrs Kapusniak. Looks a little like her, too. Infatuated, excited, thinking I would finally be understood, I told Mrs Kapusniak things.

She betrayed me.

Not at Christmas.

I don't have Christmas issues.

Therapist: Want to share the thought?

I scowl at her. She sighs.

I've recently watched a ridiculous porn flick on Kink.com in which the therapist heals the patient by, first, hypnotizing her, and then ripping off her clothes—and her own—and...

It was ridiculous. But hot.

I look at her. Anne. She's invited me to call her Anne, not Doctor What's-Her-Face. I don't know that I ever call her either. I don't say, "Oh, Anne," the way she says "Oh, Jane." Maybe I should.

Jane: Anne?

Therapist: Yes?

She's excited. She thinks I'm going to say something. Profound? I look at her again. Try to cast her in *that* role. Suppose she wanted to seduce me? How would she go about doing that?

I don't think she'd hypnotize me. She doesn't peddle hypnotherapy. Plus, fucking your hypnotized patients, probably not ethical. But if she wanted to seduce me, what would she do? Well, she couldn't be my therapist. Pretty sure that's not just unethical but illegal. I mean— not against the law-law, but against the... therapist law. Psychological law? You know what I mean. And if you don't—it doesn't matter. I know what I mean. And this is all happening inside my head.

Hmm.

So, if she wanted to be my lover—say she decided that what was wrong with me required some *deep sexual healing*—some intense fucking, all though the Christmas holidays, of course—the fucking cure instead of the talking cure, ooh, that'd be a good title for an erotic romance, no?—well, if she decided that... She'd first have to fire me, right? How would she do that?

Therapist: I'm serious, Jane. Maybe you need another therapist.

Passive-aggressively, of course. Psychologists are manipulative like that. I look at her eyes, half-obscured by thick-framed glasses—really, a precise replica of the therapist's glasses in that porn flick. Is that what's going on here? Is she trying to get me to fire her so that she can ask me out?

That's how it would play out in a sit-com.

Or a romance novel.

In a porno, we'd already be naked on the carpet—her office has no couch.

But this is real life, and so it's more complicated. Awkward. Drawn out.

But maybe?

The first few weeks, she'd say nothing when I fell silent. Try to wait me out. Now...

Therapist: Jane? You'd really get more out of this if you talked. Just a little. About anything.

I look at the rug and wonder how rough it is. Would I—would she—end up with rug burn? On her knees? On my back?

Maybe we wouldn't end up on the rug. Maybe—no, not on the desk, so fucking cliché. Against the window? I bet she has just the tiniest exhibitionism fetish. She'd get off on that, her naked breasts pressed against the cold pane of glass...

Oh. What an image. I love it.

I should write that down...

Therapist: Jane...

Jane: Could I... like, could I have some paper? And a pen?

I write, swiftly. Breasts, glass. Cold. Yes. Rug, too, for a bit. Not the desk—some fun stuff with the chair. I make a sketch. We break her glasses, but she doesn't mind.

Wait. Christmas tree. In the corner. Let's topple it. That can be part of the climax. Yes.

And somewhere in the middle of it—or at the end—I might tell her why I hate Christmas.

Or, not.

I smile.

She sees me smiling and smiles back.

Therapist: I won't ask to see it. But I'm so glad... I think that's a good first step. It makes sense. For someone like you. To get it down on paper first.

I don't laugh.

I smile, and I want to go home, and transcribe my notes and finish my story. And maybe masturbate.

Therapist: I really feel we made some progress here.

Jane: Sure. Progress. I... Yeah. I really feel... much closer to you now.

Therapist: That's wonderful. So... do you think, next week, you'll actually talk?

I smile.

Shake my head.

I'm not coming back next week. I'm firing her ass. And then, I'm going to ask her out for coffee. I expect things will progress very quickly. The first time we fuck, there will be a cold pane of glass involved. But no rug; rug burn is not sexy in life, not at all.

And maybe, eventually, spent and exhausted from sex, elated and vulnerable, I will tell her about my Christmas issues.

Mmm. Probably not.

M. Jane Colette has Christmas issues, and she deals with them obliquely in her fiction. She is not currently dating her ex-therapist. Connect with her on Twitter & Instagram at @mjanecolette and get some insight into her Christmas issues through her novels, which you can find at all the usual bookselling places and at mjanecolette.com.

LOVE LETTER

BY TIFFANY SOSTAR

*D*ear Tiffany,
　　　　Reconciling with bisexuality has been a long process.

First there was the protective unawareness of your own bisexuality—probably everyone has crushes on their friends, right? Probably everyone watches queer films and giggles and talks in hypotheticals about making out with their friends. Pretty sure. Almost certain.

Then there was marriage, and that was difficult and you tried very hard to be straight. (And many other things that you aren't. But maybe those are other stories for other times.)

And then there was the divorce. And then there was San Francisco. And then there was *that* moment on the sidewalk surrounded by people who did not assume you were straight. They didn't assume you were straight! You could feel it. The pressure lifted. People saw you, saw *you* —without seeing you *as straight*.

And then there was the coming out. Which you sort of sidled into conversations and casually dropped into text messages and social media posts, retroactively claiming your previous self into a bisexual identity that had been present... always.

Oh, didn't you know? Are you surprised? Yes, I am bisexual!
Oh, I don't know. A while. Definitely a while.

And then university.

And then queer theory.

"Cyborgs Among Us: Performing Liminal States of Sexuality" by Elizabeth Whitney. The essay that changed the course of your academic career, and your life.

Liminality!

The space between. The overlapping area in the Venn diagram. The subversive, dangerous, liberating, productive, regenerative space between and beyond.

And then you were bisexual. Fully.

Founding a community group, doing presentations, writing papers, being *out*.

But this story isn't about that.

This story is about reconciling with bisexuality, and your own bisexuality isn't the only bisexuality in your life.

So, there was the visit out East to visit your partner at law school.

And he came out to you.

You, out and proud and a community activist.

You, bisexual.

He edged up against the sharpness of his shame and confessed the great sin that had hung over him for years. The crushes on his guy friends. The fantasies. The fear.

And you held your hands out and accepted his delicate fluttering truth. It was such an honour.

And then you *freaked the entire fuck out*.

I don't mean a mild freak-out.

I mean... that one night you stayed up all night googling the likely outcome of a relationship with a bisexual man, and the Internet did *not* have hopeful news for you, and you, *you* who had read all of the academic writing on the topic published in the last ten years, you who knew the effects of stigma and the thin and toxic narratives available, you who *knew better*, you believed what you read.

He woke up one morning on winter break and you were sitting on the couch with your laptop and you had been up all night and you were tear-stained and spiralling around a panic attack that had been growing for months between that trip out East and his trip back home to Calgary. You read that male bisexuality, while possibly real, was much more likely to be a phase. You read it everywhere. You even read it on Dan Savage's blog, so that *must* mean it was true and not bi-phobic and bigoted. It was Dan Savage!

So he woke up one morning on that Christmas break and you said, "We are hiring you a male prostitute and you have to have sex with him because I need to know if you're still going to want to be with me after you've been with a guy."

And he said no, you were doing no such thing.

And you felt ashamed (as you should have—that was a horrific and abusive and *coercive* thing to have said).

And you talked a lot.

And you are lucky, Tiffany, because he didn't just break up with you right then, even though he could have. And maybe he didn't because he knew that your horrible reaction would be the same horrible reaction he would get from anyone. Maybe he stayed because he didn't think he could find anything better.

And how fucking sad is that?

But still, you're lucky.

He stayed.

And you talked it out.

You realized the stunning hypocrisy of your reaction, and learned how to breathe through the anxiety and see the toxic narratives for what they are—lies that try to control people.

And then, New Year's Eve.

It was a party. A big party.

There was burlesque.

There was dancing.

And by then, you were talking about bisexuality with more comfort, confidence.

A couple weeks is a short amount of time, but it's eons when you're in a long-distance relationship and when you're dealing with an acute issue and when you're both on winter break.

And there was this very attractive guy, and you had been flirting, both of you, with that very attractive guy, all night.

And you went and found him.

And he came over.

And you had a brief chat. (Consent is important! You learned your lesson.)

And he kissed your partner.

It was your partner's first same-sex kiss.

Eventually you had your first same-sex kiss, in a different club, on a different night, with your partner present.

Tiffany, you often feel like you have failed at being a bisexual, and definitely like you have failed at being a bisexual activist.

You still run into internalized bi-phobia. You know all the right antidotes now, but you still slam into internalized grossness on an infrequent-but-not-never basis.

You don't have enough partners, you don't have the right kind of partners, you aren't turned on by the right porn. Are you too straight? Are you just a big fake? (The answer is you have exactly the right partners, and you have great taste in porn, and you're not at all straight, and you're not a big fake. But I know you'll keep asking those questions.)

Reconciliation is a long process.

Reconciliation is a life-long process.

It's better now than it was years ago when you first

began this long journey.

There are more stories now, and I think maybe even Dan Savage has slightly changed his tune.

There is more representation.

There is still not enough.

There is still erasure.

There is still invisibility.

There is still a weird double-bind where female bisexuality is expected and accepted when it caters to straight men (it's like heterosexuality plus!), and male bisexuality is rejected and erased because they're just pausing on the way to gay.

And non-binary bisexuality is not even acknowledged.

We are all just doing the best that we can to find ourselves in the tangled mess of the cultural norms we get handed.

And we are doing the best that we can to find each other, and to hold each other's truths gently (and ideally, we are not smashing each other's truths into the solid brick wall of our own internalized bigotry, but sometimes we fuck it up).

Just keep doing your best.

I love you,

Me

Tiffany Sostar is a self-care and narrative coach with a passion for helping marginalized communities find their way to the centre of their own stories. She is a bisexual, genderqueer, neurodivergent community activist and

advocate. You can find her work at www.tiffanysostar.com and on fb.com/sostarselfcare.

EDITOR'S SHAMELESS PLUG: Tiffany Sostar, among her many talents, offers writing workshops. Write with her. It will change your life.

HOPE

BY TET MILLARE

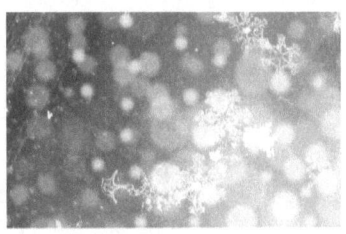

My dearest,

How are you? I hope life is treating you fairly. I'm sitting here trying to write something fun and jolly because I've been asked to write about Christmas.

Winter, December.

But it's August and hot, too early to look forward to Christmas. And I am feeling homesick. And afraid.

Today I attended a vigil for the woman who died in Charlottesville, Virginia, while protesting against a group of white supremacists. Did you see news of this back home? One of the racist dudes decided to drive into the protesters, killing her and hurting more than thirty others. I cannot believe it's 2017 and this is still happening.

But you're not in Virginia, you will say to me. You're not in the US. You're in Canada. Calgary. Utopia. Paradise.

And if not paradise—at least safe.

Well. Calgary does not feel very safe right now either. Anti-immigrant groups and white nationalists have been holding rallies here in front of our city hall. To attract people to their group, they bring food for the poor and hungry. Then they teach them the "good news." Typical, right? There should be a law against the misuse of the Bible.

Did you know that some small towns in Alberta have chapters of the KKK? I heard about them when I went on my first camping trip here, back in 2010, shortly after arriving in Canada. My friends were so worried about me camping in the bush in certain areas. They didn't want me to go but finally agreed because I told them I was going with bunch of white folks. I didn't tell you then because I didn't want you to worry about me.

And I was fine. Nothing happened.

But my friends' fear that something could have happened—that I was *not* safe—that was real. It was infectious. And living with that fear, with that awareness, it's tiring.

But you know this, right? I *think* you know this.

Here's something I got reminded of this week that does make me happy that I moved here instead of to the US: freedom of speech in Canada is *not* absolute. I totally forgot about that—but, yeah, Canada has hate-speech laws so displaying those racist symbols and actively inciting hate is not blatantly allowed here.

So, they can rant about us brown people in their homes... but not in public.

Is that progress?

You know how involved I have been with VOICES, Calgary's Coalition of Two-Spirited and Racialized LGBTQIA+? I don't know if you've been following what we've been working on lately, so let me catch you up. Remember I told you, back in April, how VOICES, together with Calgary Pride, met with the police and that the police agreed not to wear their uniforms at this year's Pride Parade? A few days ago, the official statement on this finally came out! (Yeah, four months later!) A lot of my friends were really happy about it... but the resulting media coverage and public discussions were so difficult and challenging. Progress? I suppose, but right now, I feel sad that we still need to explain all the issues, everything all over again... and again... and again. A year has already passed since we took a stand with Black Lives Matter-Toronto and I thought the community would have done its "homework" already.

But no.

Did I tell you I'm supposed to be writing about Christmas? Can I make Christmas wishes that come true year-round? Next August, next September? I suppose I can, right? So, here are my wishes for next year:

1) I do not want to get into this whole argument around police again. This isn't supposed to be about the police. This is about the lives of 2SQTBIPOC+ folks who are

constantly getting harassed and killed by institutionalized racism.

2) I know we need to talk and discuss and educate. But I'm so tired of explaining the same thing over and over again, and I wish other folks would just google the damn issue! (Thank you Wrong Kind of Girls!) To get at least a basic background, a basic level of understanding —do their homework *before* debating, engaging, arguing.

3) I want progress. Change. The kind of progress and change that comes not just from VOICES and people like us educating and doing *all* the work—but from other folks doing their homework and taking responsibility for the past, the present, and the future —creating a future in which racialized 2SQTBIPOC+ don't feel... afraid. And exhausted.

I am tired. I am really, really tired. Emotionally. Mentally. Physically.

Fighting, arguing, resisting—creating change? It's exhausting.

The good news is I haven't lost hope yet. (My psychologist confirms this, and approves.)

I am looking forward to going home in December. Yes, I will miss Christmas again this year, but hey, I will be home for both Tatay and Nanay's birthday for the first time in... I don't know... oh my... yeah... ten years. Ten years. Since I came here.

Wow.

Ok, that's it for now. I hope I won't rant too much when I get there. LOL!

Ok, I probably will.

But I'll also have hope. I promise.

See you soon! Love you!

Always,

Tet

Tet Millare is a proud queer Filipino-Canadian LGBTQIA+ advocate, community volunteer, and adventurer. One of the founders of VOICES, Calgary's Coalition of Two-Spirit and Racialized LGBTQIA+ and a board member of Fairy Tales Queer Film Fest, Tet considers herself a Jack-of-All-Trades because she has tried and will continue to try anything at least once in her life.

She strives to live life in the present and channels her hopeless sentimental side through any expression of art. Tet has written and performed (sung, even!) at the Coming Out Monologues, danced with the M:ST8 (Mountain Standard Time Performative Art), and performed as a technical non-dancer at Fluidfest. She also works as a professional photographer—check out her work on Facebook at Tet M's Photography.

EDITOR'S GLOAT: Ha! You finished! YOU ARE A PUBLISHED WRITER! Ha! Woo-hoo! Squee!

AT THE RANCH

BY PW ZELLIE

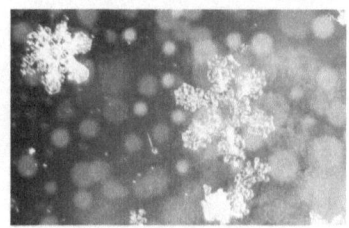

*D*ear Santa,
It's almost Christmas, and I've snuck out of yet another boring Christmas party, and here I am, hiding by the gate, writing this letter to you, hoping you can make my dreams come true.

I look to my future, but I'm conflicted. I know I should want a cowboy and sometimes I do. But mostly, I want a cowgirl.

Could there be a life with both?

Could we three live a life on a ranch? Be happy... free... *allowed*?

I am being called back to the party.

I guess I'd better go.

Maybe when I go back, I'll find my cowgirl and cowboy kissing under the mistletoe...

...and they'll beckon for me to join them.

L.

Cleverly disguised as a middle-aged nondescript librarian type, PW Zellie glides through life, unremarked upon but grinning slyly, enjoying all its yummy secrets.

A CONFESSION & A GAME: She really, really wanted to have a piece in *Queer Christmas In Cowtown*, but she didn't have time to write. At all. Nothing. But there she was, sitting across from me in the sheesha lounge. And there was my notebook. I tore a sheet out of it, and wrote three words on top of it.

"Write," I commanded. (I'm bossy.)

She wrote. This.

Your challenge, if you choose to accept it: Guess which three words I gave her. (Do it. Email the answer to TellMe@mjanecolette.com, and if you get it right, I'll send you a prezzie.)

The game, if you choose to play it: *#3littlewords* on *mjanecolette.com/3littlewords*. Check it out and write your story... three words at a time.

WARM EARS, BIG ROCK

BY ERIN SNEATH

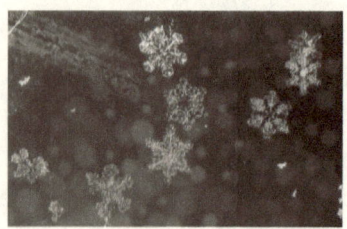

I counted any work shift with Sugar as a Christmas miracle, even when the children screamed at us, even when one of them dribbled snot on my felt costume shoes.

Sugar was lightning, electric, a brilliant beam of light in an otherwise shitty December. The crowded mall didn't feel like a mad house when she was there. She had intense eyebrows over soft stoner eyes, and the brightest dimpled smile. She kept her head covered at all times. Even when she wasn't in costume, she wore a black toque that sat so low on her head, it hid her ears. I couldn't place her accent. My dad, after he picked me up from work one night, said that she might be Finnish.

I wanted desperately to learn more about her. Her small talk, though, consisted entirely of random trivia, such as how action figures were made, or the etymology of my name (Angie), or the differences between various postal systems. She deflected most questions about herself. I didn't even guess her gender until I straight-up asked for her pronouns. Her age remained a mystery. She had a truck, but her face looked young. I hoped she wasn't too much older than I. My elf costume was mortifying enough without some pitying adult turning me down.

During our break at the food court, I asked, "Are you going anywhere Christmas Day?"

She put a finger to the perfect cupid bow of her lips. "Driving south. Hiding."

"From your family?" I casually swatted my long navy-dyed hair away from the ginger beef I was trying to eat.

"From Santa." Sugar often joked around, insinuating that we were real Christmas elves.

I gestured towards the New York Fries, where our Santa, a retired librarian named Jerry, stood in line for his double-cheese poutine.

Sugar smiled, sort of.

"Do you know why the Vikings disappeared from Greenland?" she said. "No cheese. Dairy was a staple food for them and the Arctic is a death sentence for cows."

"Can I have your contact info?" I said with phony nonchalance.

She frowned and scratched the back of her neck. "Not really."

I blanched. Conversation over. Oh god, I'd just made a fool of myself. We headed quietly to the hard foam Santa castle and took turns changing back into our costumes. She went first.

"Angie," she said through the wall. "I'm going to Big Rock tomorrow night, about eight o'clock. Want to come?"

I did a double-take. "What?"

Was she asking me out?

No.

She was humouring me.

"Big Rock: the Okotoks Erratic." She came back out, decked out from head to toe in pointy, jingle-belled felt. "Here's some trivia: did you know that—"

"Tomorrow's Christmas Eve." Offering to drive me around after refusing to give me her contact info—why was she doing that? To show off a little before disappearing from my life? That was cruel. I ducked into the castle to change before she could see the irritation on my face.

She must have sensed it. "Never mind."

The silence between us for the rest of the shift drowned out Jerry's booming "Ho Ho Ho," and all the whiney children. Then we closed for the night, along with the shops and eventually the whole mall.

I followed Sugar into the parking lot and stopped her as she climbed into her red, dented pickup. "Hold on."

I passed her a scrap of paper with my street address on it. My hand shook as much from the freezing air as it did from nervousness. The weather forecast said this cold snap would last until Boxing Day. Did Sugar really want to go sit out in the countryside at night in this kind of weather? Did she want to sit in the dark... with me?

My parents said yes (so long as I was back before midnight) but they wouldn't have if they'd seen Sugar drive. She drove as if her truck was on the downhill end of a midway ride—roller coasters don't stop at lights. How we dodged getting pulled over was beyond me. It was like no one saw us, or if they did, they didn't so much as honk. My seat belt had duct tape repairs and Sugar's high beams didn't work. I should have been scared out of my mind.

The south end of the city petered out until there were only ranches, the highway, and a bright blanket of stars in a moonless sky. If I'd been driving, I might have missed the Rock itself.

"Where I'm from, it's dark for months at a time," Sugar said. "My eyes are used to it."

We parked. The inside handle of the passenger side door had broken off long ago, so Sugar came around and helped me down as if I were a fine lady stepping out from a carriage.

"Come on," she said, "we're missing rush hour."

"Huh?" Sure, there was a bit of holiday traffic but hardly rush hour.

Sugar handed me a pair of gloves to wear, with grip pads on the palm and fingers. Ignoring the "Do Not Climb" signs, I followed her the nine meters up to the boulder's flat top, even as the chill threatened to stiffen my fingers into uselessness.

She lay down and patted the space to her right, inviting me to join her.

I can't describe the Milky Way as I saw it through the driest prairie air, away from city lights. I can't tell you whether the prickling of tears in my eyes was a reaction to the beauty above me, the beauty beside me, or the biting cold.

"Take off your glove," Sugar said. She tapped my hand, the one nearest her.

"My hand will go numb."

"Trust me."

The way I trusted her driving?

I obeyed. Sugar took my naked hand in hers. Her hand felt hot, her pulse emphatic. How? Did she climb with the world's best gloves on and removed them when I wasn't looking, or did she somehow climb barehanded without even cooling down?

She said, "Can you see them?"

"The stars? Breathtaking," I said, my breath forming a white cloud.

"No. I mean rush hour, everybody heading north at the same time because the big man said so. It's what we do, Santa's little freaking helpers. This year, I sent my naughty *versus* nice intel with a colleague. I'm sending a letter of resignation too, though I doubt anyone will believe that I'm serious. My life until now had exactly one purpose. I've had enough."

She sounded like she'd rehearsed this speech, and not necessarily for me.

"Enough of life?" Is that why she wouldn't keep in touch? Oh god...

She chuckled. "Of not making my own choices, Angie. Here."

She let go of my hand and fumbled around in her pocket. My hand started to freeze almost immediately. I barely felt the envelope she pressed into my palm.

I strained my eyes in the dark as I tore it open.

Sugar said, "It's what you wanted for Christmas. It's not from Santa, it's not from your parents, it's from me."

My heart stopped. It was a ticket, to *Night Vale: The Musical*. I squealed like a child.

"I never told you I wanted to go to this," I said. "I never told anyone."

She said, "And yet I heard you."

I sat up and looked at Sugar, really looked at her through the dark.

I said, "These cost a ton. It's a sold-out show. How?"

She took off her hat. She had terrible hat-hair, which didn't surprise me, but the sight of her ears changed my universe.

"Can..." My voice cracked. "Can I touch them?"

She rose and put her forehead against mine. "They're sensitive, especially this time of year."

Sugar's ears radiated heat. They vibrated like a television speaker. I gently traced my fingers from her earlobes, pierced many times over, to their pointed elfin tips. My fingers tingled. Then again, so did everything else.

There was no way I was willing to take off my coat or my snow pants on the Big Rock at -24C. We went to her truck. We stayed parked for a long time. I nearly missed my curfew.

And then, Sugar was gone. Me... I'm here. Working as an elf again this Christmas. Saving money. When I can afford it, I'll head south in search of a girl with an accent... a runaway with intense brows over mellow eyes who covers her ears with a toque, drives like a maniac, hides from Santa, and knows exactly what I want for Christmas.

Erin Sneath likes her holiday stories the way she likes potato latkes, piping hot. Despite all January resolutions, she runs darkly madcap the rest of the year. She sometimes goes by Spooky Flashlight at erinsneath.com and on Twitter she's @erinsneath. She also writes TerribleTarot.com, a loving spoof of Tarot handbooks. You can read more of her stories in the Enigma Front anthologies, available at Amazon and at Calgary's own Sentry Box.

EDITOR'S PONTIFICATION: I believe in elves, and I think I dated one once, so please don't tell me that this story is fiction. It doesn't just *sound* true, it could be true. More importantly: it *reads* true. Fiction, non-fiction... all good stories *read* true.

ANTICIPATING DISAPPOINTMENT

BY MARZENA CZARNECKA

*D*ear Santa,

You didn't deliver last year's Christmas present to me until this July, and when it finally came, it was bitter, almost foul, and not the sweet treat I had asked for.

I'm trying to be grateful for it anyway... but it's hard.

I'm mostly resentful.

I guess it's not your fault.

I *know* it's not your fault.

I'm not even going to ask you to make it up to me this year. I'll get over... the disappointment. And I suppose you fulfilled the letter of our contract... if not the spirit.

Hey, I said I'm *trying* to be grateful. But... I'm resentful. Could you do better this year?

I think... I'd like you to read my mind. I'd like to get what I want without asking for it. Partly because... asking for shit is so fucking hard. I don't want to do it anymore. I just want... to get what I want without asking for it.

What? I don't deserve a little bit of entitlement at Christmas?

Don't tell me you're not a mind reader. You're Santa Claus, for fuck's sake. A saint of sorts, right? A demi-god, really, perhaps even a full god in our crass commercial pantheon. All-powerful, all-knowing, right?

So this year... just give me what I want. The real thing, not some warped, slap-me-upside-the-head, ironic version.

Okay?

Thanks.

M.

PS I'm imagining your face and response when you get this letter... and I'm already anticipating feeling disappointed. So if I'm anticipating being disappointed, when Christmas comes and my present arrives—or doesn't—will you have actually given me what I expect?

Don't be... don't be like that.

Please.

Don't give me what I expect.

Give me what I want.

Marzena Czarnecka fully expects Santa to screw her over again this year. You can find her creative non-fiction at NothingByTheBook.com and her legacy business writing portfolio at CalgaryBusinessWriter.com. She talks in pictures on Instagram as NothingByTheBook.

A CHALLENGE TO YOU: Want to write something for next year's *Queer Christmas in Cowtown* but don't know where to start? Start here—a letter to Santa. Maybe, at the end, it will be just a letter to Santa, a self-indulgent whine that doesn't really go anywhere. That's fine. It will still be—it will *be* written. Finished. And that's awesome.

But maybe... it will start you thinking. About another letter to Santa. A future letter to Santa. A letter to someone else. Her. Him. Them. That time... and you'll start writing *that* story, and writing that story is going to change the life of someone who reads it.

Maybe.

That's what happens.

So. What are you waiting for? Pen. Paper. Or—fingers. Keypad. And... go.

"Dear Santa..."

Your deadline is July 31, 2018.

ABOUT YYC QUEER WRITERS

Queer Christmas in Cowtown is the second collaborative project by YYC Queer Writers, formed in 2013 by writer and activist Dallas Barnes. We get together intermittently to... write. Also, laud our lovers. Commiserate about our exes. Share what we wrote. Explain what we want to write. Try to justify why we aren't writing it. Go home and write it. Come back. Share it... repeat.

We believe telling and sharing stories is how we change the world.

In YYC and want to write with us? Find us on Facebook at Calgary Queer Writing Group or send us a note through *mjanecolette.com/yycqueerwriters*.

MORE PROJECTS

BY YYC QUEER WRITERS

- *Screw Chocolate: 14 QUEER valentines to get you through February 14,* February 2017
- *Screw Chocolate 2,* coming February 2018
- *Queer Christmas In Cowtown*: theme to be determined, coming December 2018

Interested in contributing? Go to *mjanecolette.com/yycqueerwriters* for details.